Nine Stories:
A Reader's Guide to the J.D. Salinger Story Collection

ROBERT CRAYOLA

CONTENTS

INTRODUCTION

This guide to J.D. Salinger's *Nine Stories* (published as *For Esmé - with Love and Squalor, and Other Stories* in many countries) will add to your understanding of the book and get you thinking about its deeper dimensions. We will examine it from a variety of angles and this will be beneficial whether you are totally new to the book or have already familiarized yourself with the text.

Following publication of *The Catcher in the Rye* in 1951, J.D. Salinger was one of the most acclaimed and successful writers of his time. His fans eagerly awaited a new work. The release of *Nine Stories* in 1953 didn't quite fit the bill – all of the stories had previously been published in magazine form – but they made the stories available to a wider audience. The collection met with great success and contains some of his most well-known works.

Let's begin our study by looking at the author of *Nine Stories*, J.D. Salinger.

AUTHOR: Jerome David Salinger was born in New York City on January 1, 1919. He was raised Jewish but would later learn that his mother wasn't actually Jewish. He published in school newspapers growing up and was socially active in numerous clubs.

After high school, he began college at NYU but soon dropped out. He tried to make it in the meat-packing industry, even going to

Austria for the business, but he quickly returned just before the Nazis annexed Austria.

He began college once more in Pennsylvania and again dropped out. He continued writing, however, and took a writing class at Columbia University. He had his first story professionally published in *Story* magazine in 1940. He would submit stories to *The New Yorker* and finally had "Slight Rebellion off Madison" accepted, but because of the war references, it was not published until 1946. It featured the character of Holden Caulfield, later the narrator in *The Catcher in the Rye*.

In 1942 Salinger was drafted and served active duty during several major battles. While in Europe, he arranged to meet Ernest Hemingway, whom he respected. Hemingway saw great promise in the young writer and encouraged him.

Salinger continued to write and submit stories during the war, but he suffered a great deal of traumatic stress. When the war ended, he married a German woman and returned with her to the U.S. The marriage failed after eight months and she returned to Germany.

Salinger tried to have a book of stories published at this time, but the deal fell through. He continued to write and publish, and with the publication in *The New Yorker* of "A Perfect Day for Bananafish" he secured a contract with the magazine that gave them first-rights to publish his stories. He would release short works mainly through them for the remainder of his career. The story would mark the first appearance of the Glass family, and Salinger would use them in numerous other stories.

About this time, he also took a strong interest in Zen Buddhism. It would be the first of many schools of thought to interest him. He would take his practices very seriously and often encourage or force others close to him to adhere to his systems.

In an attempt to secure more money, Salinger sold the film rights of a story to Hollywood and they turned it into *My Foolish*

Heart. He hated the film and vowed to never have one of his works mutilated in that way again.

In the late 40s Salinger began work on his first novel, *The Catcher in the Rye.* It featured Holden Caulfield from his earlier story and was a semi-autobiographical tale of a disaffected youth. It would be published in 1951 to enormous success, earning critical acclaim, banned in some countries and schools, and still selling about 250,000 copies a year to this day.

A second book followed in 1955: *Nine Stories,* collecting a variety of material. It was also successful. Salinger's growing fame was unwelcome, and he moved from New York to New Hampshire and began to live a more reclusive lifestyle, also publishing less. He married in 1955 and had two children before divorcing in 1967. He would publish his final two books in the early 1960s: *Franny and Zooey,* and *Raise High the Roof Beam, Carpenters and Seymour: An Introduction.* His final published work was a novella in 1965.

Salinger's home life is reported as being regimented and peculiar. It's hard to say how accurate these descriptions are. They mainly come from writer Joyce Maynard, who had a 9-month relationship with Salinger in 1972 when she was 18 and he was 53, and his daughter Margaret Salinger. Scrutiny in the reclusive author didn't abate. His son would denounce the viewpoint told by Salinger's daughter in her memoir, leaving many questions unanswered. Salinger died on January 27, 2010 at age 91, and interest by fans continues to this day with the release of the documentary *Salinger.*

CONTEXT: We should keep the book's era in mind when we read it. The stories in *Nine Stories* take place in the late 1940s and early 1950s, when America was beginning to experience a new prosperity. People had returned from World War II and wanted a safe family life, the American dream of a home and steady work. Much of this was harshly derided by Holden Caulfield in *The Catcher in the Rye,* and that dream will be further dissected in these stories.

THE ELEMENTS
OF LITERATURE

STRUCTURE: As the title says, the book is divided into nine stories. Although not directly related, some of the stories use the Glass family, a series of characters Salinger would also use in two other books and a novella.

The first and last stories also serve as counterpoints on the subject of death. One features the suicide of a middle-aged man, and the other features the apparent death of a child. How they each approach death shows Salinger's own interest in spirituality.

SETTING: Most of the stories take place in the United States, primarily New England. The settings also include Florida and Europe.

NARRATOR & P.O.V.: Some of the stories are narrated in the first-person voice, and some in the third-person limited. This second perspective often leaves many questions unanswered.

TENSE: The stories are written in the past tense.

TONE: Tone is how a book "feels." Many of the stories have a dry or dark sense of humor, yet there is an underlying sadness to much of the work.

CONFLICT: Conflict is the struggle faced by the characters.

Much of the conflict is focused on the relationships of people (friends, lovers, etc.). There is also a good deal of internal conflict as characters struggle to find meaning in life.

THEMES: Themes are what the author chooses to illustrate through the narrative. Some of the themes in the stories include:

The Search for Authenticity – Many characters struggle to live a life of greater meaning and more in touch with who they are.

Overcoming Self-Deception – The narrator in "De Daumier-Smith's Blue Period" and the older man in "Pretty Mouth and Green My Eyes" both must confront their actions and decide if they are doing the right thing.

The Emptiness of the American Dream – Characters who seem successful on the outside (Seymour in "A Perfect Day for Bananafish" and Eloise in "Uncle Wiggily in Connecticut") have breakdowns and show that achieving the American Dream is not all it's cracked up to be.

Nostalgia – "The Laughing Man" and "For Esmé – with Love and Squalor" have narrators looking back on key memories in their life.

STORY SUMMARIES
& COMMENTARY

"A PERFECT DAY FOR BANANAFISH"

First published: January 31, 1948 in *The New Yorker*

The opening story introduces the Glass family, although little connection is made to the other members of the family in this tale. Seymour Glass, the oldest sibling, is on vacation with his wife Muriel in Florida. The first part of the story consists of a phone call. Muriel is alone in her hotel room when the phone rings. We're given hints in Salinger's description that Muriel is very pretty, somewhat shallow, and that she has always had a great deal of admirers. She seems more interested in grooming herself than in answering the phone, but eventually she picks it up.

The person phoning her is Muriel's mother in New York. Muriel's mother is very concerned about her daughter. The mother comes off as overexcited and nervous, but later we'll see that her concern is justified. Throughout the conversation between mother and daughter we are given hints about Seymour. Muriel's mother makes him sound extremely peculiar. She says he is unstable. We learn that Seymour was released from an army hospital after World War II, and that he is very intelligent. Muriel's mother has also spoken with a psychiatrist (psychiatry was very popular in the 1940s and 50s) who is convinced Seymour could "lose control of himself" at any time. She is amazed that Muriel allowed Seymour to drive the car.

They talk about other things like fashion and avoiding sunburn at the beach (Muriel received a bad sunburn), but the talk keeps returning to Seymour. As readers who haven't yet met Seymour, this builds a sense of anticipation for when we actually do see him. In what way will he be "peculiar"?

Seymour has been spending his vacation time in Florida on the beach or playing piano. These are activities we might consider normal and relaxing, so there doesn't seem cause for concern. Muriel ends the call unconcerned, but promises to call her mother if Seymour does or says anything unusual.

The second section in the story has a large shift in tone (how the story *feels*). A very young girl named Sybil Carpenter is at the beach with her mother. Sybil seems obsessed with Seymour Glass (she keeps saying "see more glass"), and her mother leaves her on the beach to play while she returns to the hotel for a martini with her friend.

Sybil goes up the beach and finds Seymour. When they talk, Seymour has a very humorous manner of speaking that amuses young Sybil. The girl asks Seymour where "the lady" is, referring to Muriel, his wife. By referring to Muriel as "the lady" Sybil shows that Muriel belongs to the world of adults and is disliked. Seymour, on the other hand, has the child's sympathy and admiration and he seems to thrive in the world of children. Seymour often talks beyond the range of Sybil's knowledge (he asks her astrological sign, for instance), but she doesn't seem to mind. Their conversation jumps from topic to topic, and Seymour gladly goes along with it, keeping it silly. Sybil, who probably has a crush on him, seems jealous of Seymour's attention to another little girl at their hotel.

They go in the water and Seymour says they'll try to find a bananafish. This is clearly a fictitious fish, but young Sybil isn't aware of that. Seymour gives a detailed description of a bananafish and says they can eat up to 78 bananas. We as readers can suppose he's only playing make-believe with Sybil. But we might also be thinking of his wife Muriel's conversation with her mother. Is it possible that Seymour can't distinguish between his imagination and reality? This doesn't seem to be the case, but we might wonder. The fact that Seymour says it's a "perfect" day for bananafish might also cause us to consider what is special about that day.

Needless to say, they don't find a bananafish in the water, and after riding a few waves on her float, Sybil and Seymour return to the shore. Sybil leaves without looking back.

The story ends with Seymour returning to his hotel. In the elevator, he angrily accuses a woman of looking at his feet. He seems paranoid, overexcited, and humorless, a harsh contrast to his demeanor around Sybil.

He goes to his room and finds Muriel asleep in bed. Then, the twist ending of the story: He takes his gun out from his drawer and blows his brains out. This is so unexpected that the reader is almost forced to reread the story to learn what has happened. Why has Seymour suddenly killed himself? A close examination can provide clues, but no definite answer.

We know from the earlier phone conversation that Seymour has been behaving strangely since the war. Nowadays we might call it PTSD (Posttraumatic stress disorder). His wife and mother-in-law have both noticed it and are concerned, but his wife has less concern. When we see Seymour for the first time he seems all right. He enjoys playing on the beach with Sybil. It's only when he leaves the world of children and goes back to the adult world that we realize something's wrong. He can't deal with the harsh realities of adulthood, and he takes things the wrong way.

We could get a deeper analysis of Seymour if we saw more of him (and Salinger offers more details in his other books), but there is enough in the story itself to indicate Seymour's unsettled feelings in the adult world. Since many men had returned from World War II at the time of the story's publication, we can guess they could relate to the feelings involved when coming back to "normal" life after the war.

"UNCLE WIGGILY IN CONNECTICUT"

First published: March 20, 1948 in *The New Yorker*

The second story in *Nine Stories* can be seen as the flip side of the first story. Instead of entering the world of children, this story looks at an adult woman who does *not* commit suicide, but who has nevertheless attained a tragic existence.

The story takes place on a cold snowy day in Connecticut. Eloise Wengler lives in an upper class neighborhood with her husband Lew, daughter Ramona, and the maid Grace. Her friend from college, Mary Jane, a divorcée, has driven up to visit her. Mary Jane had initiated the visit with a phone call, but Eloise clearly needs someone to talk to. Her life in the large house seems empty. Eloise has more money than Mary Jane, but they can still relate to each other because of their college experiences.

The two women get down to drinking, smoking, and gossiping about people they knew in college. Mary Jane wants to leave after a while — she has to work as a secretary part of the day — but Eloise insists that she stay. They gossip more and seem like very shallow women. Eloise also criticizes her black maid Grace, who she says is reading *The Robe* (a popular historical novel about early Christianity) instead of serving them.

Eloise's daughter Ramona comes home from school. She has to wear thick glasses to see and has poor social skills. There aren't any other children in the neighborhood she can play with and this has forced her to create an imaginary friend, Jimmy Jimmereeno. Mary Jane, without any children of her own, finds this incredible. Eloise, long used to it, is less amused.

Mary Jane wants to leave so she can work but it's clear both women are drunk. She's also worried her car won't start as the weather has grown colder. Eloise convinces her to phone her boss with an excuse. "Say you're dead," says Eloise.

They talk some more. Before Eloise met her husband, she knew a man named Walt, and she loved him. This is actually Walter Glass, brother to Seymour from "A Perfect Day for Bananafish," although that isn't made clear in either of the two stories and we only know it from later books Salinger wrote. As the two women drink and smoke excessively, Eloise talks about a day they were running for a bus and she sprained her ankle. Walt said, "Poor Uncle Wiggily," and his humor and gentleness has always stayed with her. We see that her current life is desperately spent reminiscing, that she doesn't love her husband the way she loved Walt, and that she is disconnected from her daughter. She is obsessed with status, and misses genuine laughter and experience.

Eloise tells Mary Jane that husbands are all jealous. Eloise has harsh criticism for her husband Lew. She says he pretended to like Jane Austen's books but he hasn't even read them.

We learn that her previous lover Walt was killed, but Eloise has never told Mary Jane how. It was during World War II, but Walt wasn't killed in action. After enough drinks Eloise finally explains. Walt was packing a Japanese stove to be mailed back to the U.S. and the stove exploded, killing him and injuring another man.

Eloise is strongly affected by telling the story and cries. She asks

Mary Jane to instruct the maid to give Ramona an early dinner. Mary Jane goes to do so, but comes back with Ramona instead. Grace was in the bathroom and it seems likely that Ramona overheard the end of the women's conversation (based on what she does next). Ramona reveals that her imaginary friend Jimmy has been run over and killed by a car. Mary Jane finds it amusing but Eloise is disturbed and sends Ramona upstairs to eat her supper.

The echo of Eloise's story in the death of Ramona's imaginary friend indicates that Ramona could have overheard her mother's story and sought to emulate it. Why she would do this is unknown (if indeed she overheard her mother), but perhaps she wished to show a kind of sympathy and connection to her mother, as many children do.

The women drink some more and pass out on the couch. At 7:05 p.m. the phone rings. Eloise answers and it's Lew. He wants Eloise to pick him up in the car, but she says she's blocked in by Mary Jane's car and they can't find the key. It seems more likely that she's just too drunk and doesn't care about picking her husband up. It's clear she is not eager to do him any favors, and she suggests he finds a ride with others.

Grace, the maid, asks if her husband (who is visiting) can stay the night in her room because of the heavy snow. Eloise sternly refuses, saying that she isn't running a hotel (although it seems likely Mary Jane may spend the night). This shows how callous Eloise has become.

Still drunk, Eloise checks on Ramona. Her daughter is napping and has left room on her bed for her imaginary friend. Eloise asks her why there's a space if Jimmy has been killed. Ramona says it is for "Mickey Mickeranno," her *new* imaginary friend. Like her mother, Ramona has quickly filled the place of her dead boyfriend. This angers Eloise and she forces Ramona to move to the center of the bed and close her eyes. At this point it's obvious that Eloise is a miserable woman. She picks up her daughter's thick glasses, says,

"Poor Uncle Wiggily," and seems to be thinking of her life as it might have been.

Ramona's crying brings Eloise back to reality. She kisses her daughter (showing she still has some heart in her). Then she goes to Mary Jane and asks about a criticism brought against her dresses while in college and asks, "I was a nice girl, wasn't I?"

This ending brings together all the strands that have told us this is a woman living in a world of emptiness and approval, living in the past because she can't bear to be in the present. It is a portrait more than anything, and there are no easy "solutions" to her problems.

"JUST BEFORE THE WAR WITH THE ESKIMOS"

First published: June 5, 1948 in *The New Yorker*

Ginnie Mannox and Selena Graff are classmates who play tennis together. Although friends, Ginnie resents Selena for always leaving her to pay the taxi fare on the way home. Ginnie is 5' 9", and 15 years old.

Finally fed up with paying the taxi fare, she tells Selena that she owes her $1.90 and she needs it that night for the movies. Selena acts surprised and slighted. The girls hardly seem like friends. Selena says her mother has pneumonia, tries to look like a sympathetic victim, but Ginnie refuses to back down, following Selena into the house to collect the money. Selena says, "I never in my life would've though you could be so small about anything," and goes to wake her mother to pay Ginnie.

While Ginnie waits in the living room, Selena's brother Franklin meets her. He is in his pajamas, has a scraggly beard growth, and looks like he just woke up. He is like an awkward boy-man, and he has cut his finger somehow. He heard someone in the living room and came out to see if it was his friend Eric.

Franklin knows Ginnie's sister Joan and calls her a "goddam snob." Ginnie defends her sister and tells Franklin that Joan is engaged. He pretends to be disinterested but it turns out he wrote Joan eight letters (which she ignored), so he clearly liked her.

Perturbed about his cut, Ginnie suggests he put iodine on it. He offers her a chicken sandwich. Despite his apparent grumpiness, he wants to do something for Ginnie. He smokes and tries to act like an adult. He tells Ginnie how he worked in an airplane factory in Ohio and that he has a bad heart.

He looks outside at men racing around and says they're going to the draft board, and that the next war will be with the Eskimos and only men around 60 can enlist. Ginnie tries to follow his whimsical train of thought but realizes she might have insulted him when she says he won't have to enlist, reminding him that he couldn't fight in World War II with his bad heart.

Franklin finally leaves to shave and tells Ginnie that should his friend Eric arrive he will be fast. He quickly returns with the sandwich, however, and waits for Ginnie to take a bite. She doesn't really want to but she eats a little.

Soon Franklin's friend Eric arrives. He is in his "early thirties" and complains about the bad morning he's had (both Franklin and Eric and pessimistic), harping on the writer roommate he has.

He compliments Ginnie on her coat and asks her name, but she avoids giving it. He seems like a vain man. He's going with Franklin to see Jean Cocteau's *Beauty and the Beast*. Both men worked in the same airplane factory in World War II.

Selena returns. Ginnie suddenly reverses what she said earlier. She tells Selena she doesn't want the money; Selena always brings tennis balls and that's compensation enough. Selena doesn't understand. In reality, Ginnie wants to save face in front of the men she's met. They've taken an active interest in her and she wants to look good to them, not petty.

Ginnie asks Selena about Franklin and she tells her he recently quit his job and feels he's too old (24) to return to college.

Ginnie leaves. The conversation with the two men (especially Franklin) has given her much to think about. She still has the sandwich Franklin gave her. She wants to throw it away but can't. She keeps it in her back pocket and the story ends with this thought: "A few years before, it had taken her three days to dispose of the Easter chick she had found dead on the sawdust in the bottom of her wastebasket."

Some critics have taken the Easter reference to mean that Franklin is a Christ figure, somehow offering a kind of "salvation" to Ginnie. It certainly isn't in any religious sense, and his unwanted chicken sandwich cannot be anything but a token of affection. If Franklin represents anything, it is a doorway out of the monotony in Ginnie's life. Like many Salinger characters, she can barely recognize how empty her life is until she meets someone like Franklin, an odd character who takes an interest in her. Although she is slightly repulsed by Franklin, she is also fascinated with the eccentricity he represents.

"THE LAUGHING MAN"

First published: March 19, 1949 in *The New Yorker*

Set in 1928 when the narrator is nine, "The Laughing Man" is a fascinating mix of nostalgia, pulpy radio serials, and youthful innocence. The narrator is too young at the time to fully comprehend all the events that take place, but we as readers can make educated guesses about the missing pieces of the story (like many of Salinger's stories).

The unnamed narrator is part of "The Comanche Club," a boys' after-school program led by a man called "Chief" (his real name is John Gedsudski). The club mainly plays sports in Central Park in New York, also going to museums on rainy days, and playing more sports and camping on weekends.

The narrator's admiration of Chief is a central part of the story. Chief is about 22 or 23, a law student at NYU, stocky, and highly loved and respected by the boys. Aside from being a great guy, Chief also regularly tells the boys a story about "The Laughing Man." This story is reminiscent of radio serials and pulp fiction, lurid tales of suspense and mystery that seem to go on forever.

The protagonist of this story-within-the-story, the Laughing Man, is the son of a missionary couple living in China. The boy is kidnapped from his parents by bandits who try to ransom the child. The parents refused to pay the ransom and the kidnappers twisted the boy's head in a carpenters vise out of spite. The story is very exaggerated and melodramatic. The Laughing Man has a horrible face and wears a mask to hide it. He was raised by the bandits, but talked to animals and regularly communed with nature. When he began to outdo the bandits in deeds, they loathed him, and tried to kill him, but failed.

In the story, China borders France, showing the ridiculous storytelling style of Chief, stringing things together however they might fit. The Laughing Man's enemy is the detective Marcel Dufarge and his daughter. He leaves clues for them in the sewer system of Paris. But although the Laughing Man steals, he donates money to monks. He lives with a band of outcasts.

The boys in the Comanche club (including the narrator) idolize the Laughing man. All 25 of the boys view themselves as "descendents" of the Laughing Man, acting as heirs or accomplices in a secret society.

One day, the boys on the bus notice that Chief has put a picture of a girl in the bus. He tells them her name is Mary Hudson. Her picture clashes with the manly decor of the bus. The boys are confused but find her beautiful. They are even more confused when Chief picks Mary up and allows her to ride the bus to the park with them. She sits next to the narrator. When they get to the park she wants to join in the baseball game. Chief discourages this, the boys are leery of the girl joining the game, but she gets her way. We overhear that she has come to town for a dentist appointment.

Chief ask the narrator to use Mary as a center fielder, which he doesn't need, but she is allowed to play. She's not very good on the field, but when she goes to bat she makes it to third base and the boys are impressed. She has won them over. In the next month she plays baseball with the boys several more times.

The Chief seems to be in a relationship with Mary. The narrator is unaware of the extent of this, but we can deduce from her regular visits that Mary and Chief are a couple. He goes to pick her up with the bus one day, and he is dressed very nice. While they wait for her, Chief tells a new installment of the Laughing Man.

Chief tells how the Laughing Man is captured by the Dufarges. He is tricked and tied up. They remove the Laughing Man's mask and Mlle. Dufarge faints when she sees his face. Marcel Dufarge fires his gun at the Laughing Man and Chief stops the story. It is a cliffhanger and the boys are intensely curious to learn the conclusion.

Chief looks at his watch and decides he can't wait for Mary any longer. He drives the boys to the park without her. The narrator asks about Mary and Chief tells the boys to be quiet.

As they play baseball the narrator notices Mary watching them from the stands. Chief goes to her and talks. The narrator tries to get Mary to play baseball but she refuses. He invites her to his house for dinner and she says, "Leave me alone." Something has changed in her demeanor.

As the narrator relates this he explains that he still doesn't know the details of what passed between Mary and Chief. As readers, we might notice the references to baby carriages. If Salinger is using these as symbols, we can speculate that perhaps she was pregnant. Chief might have dressed up nice to propose marriage, only to learn she had an abortion. We may speculate about other possibilities, but we don't have enough information to truly say.

After Mary is gone, the narrator asks Chief if he had a fight with her. Chief won't say.

When the boys are done playing baseball and back in the bus, Chief finishes the story of the Laughing Man. Chief blows his nose, clearly sad from his conversation with Mary. It is a short Laughing Man episode that he relates, and it will be the last one.

Marcel Dufarge had fired his gun and four bullets hit the Laughing Man. Two bullets went through his heart. The Dufarges approach their hated enemy and he "regurgitates" (coughs up) the bullets. This is obviously very ridiculous storytelling, but the boys appreciate it, and there is a powerful and melancholy undertone, however implausible the story may be. The Dufarges die of shock when they see the Laughing Man do this.

The Laughing Man needs eagles' blood to survive. His friend Omba brings the blood, but when the Laughing Man learns that his comrade Black Wing is dead he refuses to drink the blood and dies, removing his mask in his final gesture.

The boys are sad when they hear this ending. Some of them cry. The Laughing Man's end mirrors Chief's own sadness and signals the end of an era.

As the narrator goes home he sees a piece of red tissue paper flapping in the wind that reminds him of the Laughing Man's mask. He goes to bed in shock.

"The Laughing Man" lacks the cynicism of many of the book's stories. It is gentle, subtle, and shows a boy going through a transition and acknowledgement of the sadder aspects of life.

"DOWN AT THE DINGHY"

First published: April 1949 in *Harper's*

It's the afternoon of a hot Indian summer (a late summer, now October) near a lake. A married couple, Mr. and Mrs. Tannenbaum, and their son Lionel are vacationing at the lake, and they have two maids there with them. The maids are Mrs. Snell, who lives there year round, and Sandra, who lives in the city and is only visiting for the work.

The story begins with the two maids talking in the kitchen. Mrs. Snell has to leave to catch a bus, but she's waiting for her hot tea to cool so she can drink it. Sandra, the other maid, is worried because she said something inappropriate and the boy Lionel overheard it. She says he's always sneaking around, and although Sandra says she isn't worried, she clearly is. We don't know what she said at this point. Later we'll learn that she called Mr. Tannenbaum a "kike" (a derogatory term for a Jew). She does say at this point that the boy will have a nose like his father. Although Mrs. Snell tries to assure her that it will be all right, she also hints that Sandra might want to start looking for another job (in case she's fired).

The boy's mother comes into the kitchen. She is Boo Boo Glass Tannenbaum, another member of the Glass family. She is the sister of Seymour (who killed himself in "A Perfect Day for Bananafish") and Buddy (who died when the stove exploded, as explained in "Uncle Wiggily in Connecticut"). In this story she is 25. She is looking for food for her son, and she tells the maids how her son Lionel, although only four, has run away from home many times. Lionel is a quiet, sensitive boy, and he is easily hurt by things people say.

Boo Boo goes down to the lake and finds Lionel sitting in a dinghy (a small boat). There is no action on the lake. Everyone has left with the end of summer. Boo Boo talks to Lionel in a kind of "boy-talk." She says that she is an admiral. Lionel doesn't play along, and he's clearly dejected. He's holding something back.

Boo Boo finally addresses his current attempt to run away. She knows something happened but can't determine what it is. She tries to join Lionel in the dinghy but he won't let her on. It's a zone of privacy and comfort for him. Boo Boo tries to win him over. She has a gift key chain for him. He tells her to throw it in the lake. He's obstinate and refuses to be appeased by any gifts. He tells his mother it's his key chain so he can do what he wants with it. She finally gives it to him and he chucks it in the lake to show he's in charge. He immediately regrets this action and cries.

Boo Boo soothes him and Lionel reveals why he was running away: He overheard Sandra call his father a "big sloppy kike," and although he doesn't know what a "kike" is (he thinks it's a *kite*), he knows the remark was hurtful. Boo Boo assures Lionel that everything is okay. They make a plan to get pickles and other food at the store, and then pick up Mr. Tannenbaum at the train station and go for a boat ride.

Finally able to reveal the source of his trouble, Lionel seems better. He races with his mother back to the house and she lets him win.

Although Salinger could have made the racial slur (*kike*) and its aftermath the center of the story, he chose to focus on Lionel's feelings. The boy was hurt by the remark, the injury to people he loves, and how he copes with that injury is what drives the story. Salinger offers us the perspective of a child, and we can feel how his mother made this better not with force or logic, but with compassion and tenderness.

"FOR ESMÉ – WITH LOVE AND SQUALOR"

First published: April 8, 1950 in *The New Yorker*

One of Salinger's most popular stories, *For Esmé – with Love and Squalor, and Other Stories* is the title of non-US editions of *Nine Stories*.

This seemingly autobiographical story begins with the narrator receiving an invitation to a wedding in England from a woman who will be the focal point of this story: Esmé. She is about nineteen when he gets the invitation, but only thirteen for the events in the story.

During World War II, the narrator is enlisted in Devon, England in April of 1944. He primarily does office work. Rumors go around that the soldiers will soon be part of the D-Day landings – a massive invasion of France by Allied forces. He primarily seems bored as he waits for orders.

One rainy day, he goes into town and reads a church bulletin board and sees that children's choir practice is taking place. He goes to watch the children sing. A blond girl of about thirteen has the most noticeable voice in the group. She yawns between verses and after practice the choir director lectures her. The narrator leaves the church and goes out into the rain.

He finds a tearoom and orders tea and toast. As he drinks his tea, the girl from the choir practice comes in from the rain with her younger brother, a boy about five years old. The girl notices him and comes to speak, saying that he appeared to be lonely (which he admits).

They talk for quite a while. She is a willful young woman who intends to find success as a jazz singer and then move to Ohio (even though she has never been there). Her mother died and her father was killed in North Africa during the war. The girl wears her father's wristwatch in remembrance. She is trying to be more compassionate, and we can see the narrator admires what she will become, her varied interests, emotions, and aspirations. She eventually tells him her name is Esmé.

Esmé's brother also speaks to the narrator. He tells a childish joke and is friendly.

Esmé asks about the narrator and finds him different from other Americans she has met. When she learns he is a writer, she asks him to write a story for her, a story that includes "squalor" (something disgusting or wretched). He promises to do so, clearly affected by the mature young woman who has broken through his loneliness.

Unsure when they'll see each other again (troop movements are kept mysterious because of spies), Esmé asks if she can write the narrator. He gives her his military contact info through which she can write him wherever he is stationed. When she leaves, he describes it as "a strangely emotional moment for me." But then Esmé and her brother suddenly return. She says her brother wants to give the narrator a kiss, which he allows. Esmé makes the narrator promise once again to write her a "squalid" story.

We realize as Salinger transitions ahead in time that the story he wrote for Esmé is *the story we are reading*. He tells us that the next section will feature "the squalid, or moving, part of the story." He describes a "Sergeant X" who we immediately know is the narrator.

The narrator has changed much. The D-Day landings at Normandy have taken place and he seems to have posttraumatic stress disorder (PTSD). He doesn't open his mail. He seems to be in pain. He has trouble living each day. Without showing us the narrator's wartime experiences, Salinger *implies* that he has been through great horror and stress.

Sergeant X's friend gives us further insight into the narrator. He doesn't seem as affected by the war, and suggests (via a letter from his girlfriend back home) that Sergeant X has a psychological problem from his childhood, not the war. In the 1940s and 50s psychiatry was extremely popular, attributing most problems to "complexes" developed during infancy and childhood. Modern readers are generally more skeptical of psychiatry's all-inclusive claims, and the narrator also seems skeptical of these explanations. He is simply living in horror of what he has seen and felt during the war. His body has faced more stress than it knows how to deal with, and shakiness shows up in the narrator's facial tics and unsteady handwriting. From the narrator's conversation with his friend we see he is more intelligent and *sensitive* – a curse of many Salinger characters, who feel too deeply and don't buy into the phoniness of the world.

His friend invites him to a dance, but Sergeant X prefers to stay in. He wants to write a letter to a friend in New York. However, his hands are too shaky and he gives up. Instead, he looks in his stack of unread mail and finds a letter from Esmé. He reads it and she expresses her excitement about D-day (she wrote the letter the day after the landings). She hopes the narrator was not part of the initial assault. We can guess by his demeanor that he was. She has included her father's watch for him (the crystal in it has broken) and a greeting from her brother Charles.

The story ends with the narrator reverting to first-person. He feels "almost ecstatically sleepy," and it looks like the emptiness and darkness of his recent life is receding with the help of Esmé's letter, and he will probably make a physical recovery. As with many Salinger stories, there are islands of compassion, humor, and kindness in a sea of heartless phonies.

"PRETTY MOUTH AND GREEN MY EYES"

First published: July 14, 1951 in *The New Yorker*

This story is deceptively simple. A quick reading might lead you to think it's just about a man consoling another man over the phone. A deeper reading reveals a series of clues about what's really going on.

The story begins when Lee, a "gray-haired man" with a woman in his bed, receives a phone call in the middle of the night. The call is from his friend Arthur, an attorney, who is worried because his wife Joan still hasn't returned from a party. Lee was at the party, and Arthur was there with his wife Joan, but left without her.

Through a series of questions it becomes clear that Arthur is drunk. Lee just wants to get off the phone, but he pretends he was awake so that he can seem like a true friend to Arthur. Arthur worries that his wife left to have an affair with one of the kitchen staff. He thinks she always does that when she's drunk.

Lee tries to reassure Arthur that she probably just left with another couple, the Ellenbogens, and that she'll get home any minute now. Arthur clearly respects him and tries to take his advice, but he is very worked up in his drunken state. He berates his wife for her stupidity. They also discuss Arthur's work as an attorney, revealing Salinger's common theme about the emptiness of relentless work and the system.

Arthur returns to discussing his wife and says he should have left her. He's been with her for five years and that's too long. He refers to Lee as being unmarried, and this is a clue about the identity of the woman in his bed. If it's not his wife, we realize it might be Joan (Arthur's wife), which would make Lee very hypocritical.

Arthur concedes that there are some things he likes about Joan, and he recalls what made him fall in love with her. He remembers a poem he wrote for her that had the line, "Pretty mouth and green my eyes." Like many of Salinger's story titles, it comes from a tangent in the story, a detail that unlocks the larger whole. For if Arthur still has that feeling of love for his wife, then Lee may feel a guilt he wouldn't have otherwise experienced.

Reassuring Arthur one final time, Lee is ready to hang up the phone, when Arthur asks if he could come to Lee's for a while to talk. Lee is naturally cautious (if Joan is indeed in his bed), and puts Arthur off this plan by reminding his friend he'll want to be home when his wife arrives. They hang up.

The woman in Lee's bed (who is never named) asks questions about the call. Her curiosity seems more than is natural – unless she is in fact Arthur's wife. She applauds Lee's "performance" on the phone and they relax a little now the danger has passed.

The phone rings again. Lee quickly picks up and it's Arthur again. He informs Lee that his wife has in fact just walked in the door. Since Joan is probably right next to Lee in bed, Arthur is most likely lying, trying to put the older man's mind at rest. It's almost painful to hear Arthur lie. Joan supposedly went to get a drink with some friends after the party. Arthur also says he'll give the relationship another try with Joan. Lee puts an end to the conversation, citing a headache, and there is silence again.

Lee is irritated. He has forced a man to lie, when *he* is the one being deceitful. He drops a cigarette on the bed and the story ends uncomfortably.

The story's unsettling feeling only makes sense if Joan is in fact in Lee's bed. In an attempt to break out of their lives and problems, both Lee and Joan have created more turmoil for themselves. Lee may have fooled Arthur and gotten away with his affair, but he has created inner havoc with his conscience.

"DE DAUMIER-SMITH'S BLUE PERIOD"

First published: May 1952 in *Information World Review*

The narrator in this story is pretty full of himself. He writes in an overblown, conceited style that might initially put you off. He is a liar and fairly arrogant, but by the time the story ends he will also show some sympathetic qualities (after all, how else could we care about him?).

He was born in 1920, moved from New York to Paris in 1930 with his mother and stepfather, Bobby Agadganian, and returned to New York in 1939 with Bobby after his mother has died. He is 19 and attending art school. He claims to have won some prizes for his paintings, and this seems believable.

There seems to be an unstated conflict with his stepfather Bobby. The narrator wants to get away, and applies for a teaching job for the summer of 1940 at an art correspondence school. This is a school where the students work from home and mail in their assignments for feedback and then have the work returned to them with new assignments. Correspondence schools were common and popular for decades, and still exist (although they have largely moved from mail to the internet). He uses a fake name to apply for the job: Jean de Daumier-Smith. The school is called Les Amis Des Vieux Maîtres (The Friends of the Old Masters). He quickly puts together some commercial art samples and submits it, and is accepted as a teacher. The school is directed by M. Yoshoto in Montreal, where the narrator must travel to live and work.

The narrator takes great pleasure in telling his stepfather Bobby his plans. He tells him over dinner when Bobby has his new girlfriend with him, and the narrator imagines the girl is attracted to him and will visit him in Montreal. This kind of fantasy is common to the narrator (and other Salinger characters like Holden Caulfield).

He travels to Montreal by train and meets M. Yoshoto and his wife. He compares them both to Fu Manchu (a stereotypical Asian villain) because they are "inscrutable," and there is little conversation or clues to their character. They take the narrator to their home in the worst part of town and give him a small room without chairs. It's very basic, the pay is low, and it turns out there are no other teachers. Although the narrator has grown a mustache to pass as 29 years old, pretends to be Buddhist to please the Yoshotos, and tells endless stories about his "friend" Pablo Picasso to impress them, it seems that the Yoshotos are running as much of a scam as he is. He goes to bed that night and hears the wheezing of one of the old people through the wall. This will be a regular occurrence.

The next day he starts his job, working in a room with the old Japanese couple. He finds that they are not particularly talented artists, and although he doesn't state it directly, we can see that the school does little to help students, and is more interested in acquiring their money. The narrator's art skill isn't even enlisted that morning. All M. Yoshoto asks him to do is translate some French comments into English. The narrator does this but wonders if he'll be doing any actual art instruction.

He takes in a large amount of caffeine at lunch to make it through the day. In the afternoon, he is finally given students. The first two he harshly criticizes. In the third, however, he sees genuine talent. The student is a nun named Sister Irma. She teaches a painting class at her convent and is trying to improve on certain things.

The narrator immediately begins to fantasize about the nun. Although he hasn't seen her and doesn't know her age, he imagines her as someone his age who is pretty and approachable. His isolation has made him lonely in the school. He writes her a long letter, praising Sister Irma and describing the other students as "very retarded and chiefly stupid." He asks her for a photo, her age, and gets quite personal about her religion. He wants to visit her, and it's easy to see how his letter would offend her, overstepping the bounds of the art correspondence school as it does.

Once the letter is mailed he doesn't know how he'll survive until her next package. He's going crazy and can't smoke in the school. The new students he receives seem even worse than the other ones.

Walking around one evening, he looks in an orthopedic shop and realizes he "would always at best be a visitor in a garden of enamel urinals and bedpans, with a sightless, wooden dummy-deity standing by in a marked down rupture truss." Essentially he thinks he will always be living in a hollow world of despair. This thought frightens him and he rushes back to his room. His only hope is that he'll one day visit Sister Irma. She is 18 years old in his fantasy (we never learn her actual age).

The next day a letter arrives from the Mother Superior at Sister Irma's convent. Her art lessons with the school are to be stopped, and no real explanation is provided. The narrator is horrified. He writes a letter asking why she must stop, but he is blind to the reason: himself. He asks her repeatedly to reconsider and meet him, because he is still living under an illusion.

He doesn't mail the letter just yet. He decides to go out and get drunk first (something he says he's never done). But he doesn't drink, he just gets food and coffee. As he goes home, he passes the orthopedics shop again and sees a "hefty" woman of about 30. He stares at her and unsettles her. She falls over. He reaches out to help her but the glass separates them. This can be viewed as symbolic: The narrator is always trying to reach out to "touch" the world, but is prevented from doing so by invisible barriers.

At this time he has what he describes as a mystical experience. He feels a rush of light come upon him and he almost falls over. He goes home and realizes that he must give Sister Irma her "freedom" and let her go. He never mails his second letter to her.

Within a week, the school is closed down because they aren't licensed. The narrator doesn't seem disappointed by this. He had harshly criticized his other students when he lost Sister Irma as a pupil, and his teaching days seemed to be at an end anyway. He returns to live with his stepfather Bobby in Rhode Island until art school resumes.

He never saw or heard from Sister Irma again. One of his other students that he criticized, Bambi Kramer, found commercial success designing Christmas cards. This is an amusing twist to a sad ending.

"De Daumier-Smith's Blue Period" hinges on the narrator's attempt to outsmart everyone, to con his way to success and happiness. Only when he sees the world around him, the world that he actually experiences, and stops living in fantasy, can he have any kind of genuine contact with people.

The title's reference to a "blue period" recalls to mind Pablo Picasso's Blue Period, in which he mainly produced blue and blue-green paintings with desolate themes. The narrator lives through his own blue period in this story, but there is evidence that he will transition out of this melancholy era.

"TEDDY"

First published: January 31, 1953 in *The New Yorker*

The book's final story will hint at the content of Salinger's later books, focusing on spirituality. The title character, Teddy, is a ten-year-old boy. He has a very normal family, but claims to be reincarnated from an Indian holy man. This produces a variety of reactions from the people he meets.

The story takes place on a cruise ship. The McArdle family is returning from Europe where they had been vacation. Mr. McArdle works as an actor in the radio industry, and he is very frustrated by his family and their lack of respect toward him. His wife seems to loathe him, hinting that she'll have an affair. His six-year-old daughter Booper has run off to play with his expensive camera. And his son Teddy doesn't impress him with his mystical ways and speech.

Theodore "Teddy" McArdle appears at first glance to only be a peculiar (but intelligent) boy. The story progresses with hints Salinger gives us that the world around Teddy has taken notice of his peculiar traits. He has met with researchers in the U.S. and now Europe (on the trip). Now, if he was only a boy making audacious claims about himself that would be one thing. But Teddy claims to have the ability to make accurate predictions about the future. We're not told how accurate those predictions are, but based on the reactions of the research teams he's met we can guess that there might be some accuracy in his claims.

After introducing Teddy and his parents in their ship cabin, the boy is sent by his parents to retrieve his sister Booper. Mr. McArdle wants his camera back, and Mrs. McArdle wants to speak with Booper. Before he leaves, Teddy notes some orange peels that were thrown overboard. He says that they only exist in his mind now, and that when he leaves them it will be the same way. This may foreshadow Teddy's (possible) death at the end of the story.

On his way to find Booper, Teddy asks a female employee about a word game that is played on the ship. The woman thinks Teddy is too young for the game, but he assures her he isn't. His self-confidence about his abilities is a further hint that his isn't a typical boy.

When he finds Booper she is with another boy on the cruise, Myron. She's trying to play backgammon with him. She also seems intelligent, but lacks Teddy's compassion and maturity. She cruelly mocks Myron for not knowing how to play backgammon and tells him he'll be an orphan if his mother dies (his father died in the Korean War). Teddy sends Booper to see their parents. He wants to write in his diary and tells her they'll meet at the swimming pool at 10:30 a.m. for a lesson. Booper angrily tells Teddy she hates him and everyone on the ocean.

Next Teddy locates his reserved deck chair and opens his diary. He reads over yesterday's entry. It shows a methodical boy, considerate of others, and very inquisitive. He writes today's entry and hints that something will happen either today or on February 14, 1958, when he will be 16. Although he doesn't name the event, there are hints throughout the story that it is his death being foreshadowed.

An upbeat young man named Bob Nicholson interrupts Teddy in

his writing. He teaches at Trinity College in Dublin and is familiar with Teddy and the research being done on him. We learn the details about Teddy's talents, which sound like precognition (predicting the future). They discuss spirituality a great deal. Teddy seems almost inhuman, saying that emotions are overrated. He was making great "spiritual advancement" in India in a previous life, he goes on, until he fell from the spiritual path to love a woman. This forced him to be reincarnated in America, and being spiritual and meditating there is one of the great challenges of his existence. Teddy's parents can't truly understand him. When he was six years old he had the realization that everything is God. This is a common insight of mystical experiences, but Teddy says he's been having them since he was *four*. Teddy says that you must get rid of logic and "intellectual stuff" if you are to see things as they are. But most people are addicted to being born and dying.

To American readers of the 1950s, Eastern concepts of spirituality were still exotic and largely unknown. Salinger's interest would arouse great interest in Eastern religions and philosophy. Teddy's worldview seems largely derived from Zen Buddhism, Vedanta, and *The Gospel of Sri Ramakrishna*.

Bob Nicholson is most interested in certain predictions Teddy told the researchers. He didn't tell them the exact time of their deaths, but he hinted that they should be *careful* at those particular times. This must have been particularly unsettling (or amusing if they didn't believe Teddy), and there are stories that a recording of Teddy giving these predictions has circulated at certain parties.

In their conversation Teddy says that death isn't tragic. He says that his sister could push him into an empty swimming pool and he could fracture his skull, killing him. But it wouldn't be tragic. We might not suspect that Teddy is making a prediction about his own death at this point, and neither does Bob Nicholson.

Bob Nicholson asks Teddy for advice on improving the education system. Teddy suggests less intellectualizing early on, and a greater emphasis on experience and meditation. The unconscious can do things the conscious mind can't possibly accomplish (such as regulate cell growth), and that by surrendering to this larger intelligence anything is possible.

Teddy says he must leave for the swimming pool. He departs and Nicholson smokes his cigarette, thinking over the boy's words. Then he decides to go to the pool and see if Teddy was perhaps being serious about his offhand mention of fracturing his skull there. As he approaches the room with the pool he hears a young female voice (presumably Booper) give an "all-piercing, sustained scream" that is "highly acoustical" and reverberates through the room.

The story ends ambiguously. Did Teddy die as he described it to Bob Nicholson? That seems to be the implication. Booper presumably didn't intend to kill Teddy, but she didn't know the pool had been drained. We hear her scream when she realizes what she has done, and her scream reverberates because there is no water in the pool.

Although this seems the most plausible explanation to the scream, the story is ambiguous and other possibilities have been suggested. For example, Teddy himself hints that what he predicts is *not* definite, and that with the right information his predictions might be avoided. Some have suggested that he himself pushes Booper into the empty pool to avoid his own death. This seems unsatisfying, especially since he doesn't seem to fear death.

A further possibility is that the pool *wasn't* drained and that the scream is merely a result of play. This might be, but Salinger gives no indication of splashing sounds or water, and puts emphasis on the acoustical "reverberation." This seems to indicate no water in the pool.

The reader is invited to find his or her own interpretation, but Teddy's death as the best explanation is a haunting ending to a book that began with Seymour's death – unless we take Teddy's spiritual insight into account, in which case it is no tragedy at all.

CRITICAL QUESTIONS & ESSAY TOPICS

These critical questions are designed to get you thinking about the text and possible essay topics. I have provided suggestions in the answers below, and I encourage you to consider alternative answers as you explore these topics.

1. How does Salinger show the emptiness of life in *Nine Stories*?

Many characters reach breaking points in the stories. From Seymour's suicide in "A Perfect Day for Bananafish" to the narrator's desperate attempt to con his way to success in "De Daumier-Smith's Blue Period," characters struggle to break free of the monotony and things that hold them down. They often fail, and only seem to find meaning when they can turn to each other for help and communion.

2. What redeems life in these stories?

The characters who find meaning in these stories do so through meaningful relationships, spiritual experiences, and looking beyond the individual pettiness that has largely consumed them. Boo Boo and Lionel in "Down at the Dinghy," for instance, only find peace when Lionel stops running away and Boo Boo looks beyond her problems with the maid Sandra. They make an agreement to *find* joy together and enjoy the afternoon.

3. Why does Seymour kill himself in "A Perfect Day for Bananafish"?

Coming so unexpectedly as it does, this story almost demands that the reader go back and seek clues for Seymour's suicide. When this is done, the reader can see that Seymour has had trouble adjusting to adult civilian life and only has peace in the gentler world of play and children. There is no satisfactory "reason" for his suicide, but if one examines the story it becomes apparent that Seymour lacks a *feeling* when dealing with adults, and that his PTSD is preventing him from a lasting contentment in his daily life.

4. Why does Ramona's imaginary friend Jimmy die in "Uncle Wiggily in Connecticut"?

Although not explicitly stated, it seems very probable that Ramona overheard her mother Eloise tell Mary Jane about the death of her boyfriend Buddy. Like many children, she imitates her parents. This is a little too personal for Eloise, however, and the memory devastates her. The story's focus is really on Eloise, and the cause of Ramona's imitation isn't too important. It merely serves to uncover an old wound that Eloise hasn't addressed – not by covering it up with a new husband and house. She has drowned herself in alcohol and it has negatively affected her treatment of her maid and her daughter.

5. In "Just Before the War with the Eskimos," what is Ginnie's interest in Franklin?

Since she seems largely repulsed by Franklin, why does Ginnie want to return to Selena's house? This probably stems from her confusion about Franklin. She finds his physical demeanor initially unattractive, but something inside her responds to his interest and kindness. Like much attraction, it may not be immediately apparent at a conscious level, or she may not be ready to admit it yet. Whether it's an attraction she will actually *pursue* is questionable. He's 24 and she's 15, after all.

It could also be argued that she's not attracted to him, that she just finds him peculiar and different from the rest of the people she knows. Either way, she is intrigued.

6. Why doesn't Salinger reveal the nature of Chief and Mary's relationship problems in "The Laughing Man"?

Since the narrator is nine years old, Salinger preserves a sense of innocence in the story. He doesn't need to know the exact details of their relationship to know that something has gone awry. Both Chief and Mary seem sad, and that affects the Laughing Man narrative Chief tells as well. We can make our guesses about Chief and Mary's relationship, but it won't affect the sense of loss that the characters feel, and which Chief suggests so skillfully in his sudden end to the Laughing Man serial.

7. How does the narrative focus shift in "Down at the Dinghy"?

The narrative shifts its focus from the maids and Sandra's dilemma to Lionel, and his unknown problem. Boo Boo talks to him and learns that he is distressed by what Sandra has said, but rather than "solving" the problem and firing Sandra right away, she focuses on helping Lionel and finding harmony as a family. Salinger has chosen a "feminine" resolution rather than the sharp backlash we might have expected. This motherly ending is more satisfying, and shows that a narrative doesn't need to tie up loose ends and answer every question to be effective.

8. Why does Esmé want a story with *squalor* in "For Esmé - with Love and Squalor"? How does Salinger satisfy her?

Esmé seems to want a story that relates to her own life, the struggle she has known as an orphan during World War II, acting as a parent figure for her brother and trying to find her own escape through dreams of becoming a famous singer.

Salinger's attempt to give her a story is composed of both her own narrative and the ensuing events that take over his life (in the war). Even as Salinger struggles with PTSD following the Normandy landings, he shows that his trauma has been eased by the memory made on a single afternoon. Esmé and her brother are a memory he turns to for some comfort.

9. In "Pretty Mouth and Green My Eyes," why does Arthur call Lee a second time and lie to home about his wife coming home?

If we imagine Arthur once he ends his first call to Lee, we might guess he is embarrassed by the drunken late-night call to his friend. Arthur realizes he has burdened Lee with his problems that he assumes don't really concern the older man. Feeling guilty, he probably decided to call back and put his friend's mind at ease about Joan's safety and Arthur's own peace of mind. The irony, of course, is that his lie has the potential to irritate Lee's conscience about sleeping with the other man's wife, since Lee knows he has forced Arthur to pretend to be something he is not.

10. In "De Daumier-Smith's Blue Period," why doesn't the narrator mail his letter of inquiry to Sister Irma?

The narrator's mystical experience outside the orthopedics shop seems to be the cause for the narrator's change of heart. We can speculate about the exact nature of the experience – he is vague about it – but its occurrence at the same spot where he felt despair on another night is not coincidental. He seems to recognize that he is the one generating meaning about Sister Irma, that he really doesn't have enough information for her to be anything but a creature of his mind. As such, he seems to have an epiphany near the orthopedics shop, a counterpoint to his experience of despair. There is no reason for him to pursue a fantasy.

11. Is "Teddy" a tragedy?

In the classical sense, a *tragedy* is defined as a story that ends with a character failing or dying due to a tragic flaw. "Teddy" doesn't seem to fit this definition, since there is no tragic flaw that destroys Teddy (taking the view that he has died). Nor does he seem to view his own death as tragic. The story almost gives the reader the perspective of Teddy, that death is no tragedy, just something that happens. "Teddy" steps beyond classical narrative resolution, making itself both unsettling and satisfying.

CONCLUSION

Nine Stories covers a wide range of characters, topics, settings, and themes. It shows a broader picture of what Salinger can do with narrative than any of his other books, and its stories hold up well to multiple readings and different perspectives. I hope this guide has helped you navigate this book, and deepened your understanding of all that occurs in its pages.

Made in the USA
Las Vegas, NV
23 October 2023

79584819R00031